Thinking Critically: Cell Phones

Other titles in the Thinking Critically series:

Thinking Critically: Cell Phones

Carla Mooney

ReferencePoint Press®

San Diego, CA

For more information, contact:
ReferencePoint Press, Inc.
PO Box 27779
San Diego, CA 92198
www.ReferencePointPress.com

Cover credit: Thinkstock Images
Steve Zmina: 10, 17, 24, 31, 36, 41, 46, 55, 60

LIBRARY OF CONGRESS CATALOGING-IN-PUBLICATION DATA

Mooney, Carla, 1970-
  Thinking critically: cell phones / by Carla Mooney.
    pages cm. -- (Thinking critically)
  Includes bibliographical references and index.
  ISBN-13: 978-1-60152-580-2 (hardback)
  ISBN-10: 1-60152-580-X (hardback)
  1. Cell phones and teenagers--Juvenile literature. 2. Cell phones--Social aspects--Juvenile literature. I. Title. II. Title: Cell phones.
  HQ799.2.C45.M66 2014
  303.48'33--dc23
                                                    2013011853

Contents

Foreword

"Literacy is the most basic currency of the knowledge economy we're living in today." Barack Obama (at the time a senator from Illinois) spoke these words during a 2005 speech before the American Library Association. One question raised by this statement is: What does it mean to be a literate person in the twenty-first century?

E.D. Hirsch Jr., author of *Cultural Literacy: What Every American Needs to Know*, answers the question this way: "To be culturally literate is to possess the basic information needed to thrive in the modern world. The breadth of the information is great, extending over the major domains of human activity from sports to science."

But literacy in the twenty-first century goes beyond the accumulation of knowledge gained through study and experience and expanded over time. Now more than ever literacy requires the ability to sift through and evaluate vast amounts of information and, as the authors of the Common Core State Standards state, to "demonstrate the cogent reasoning and use of evidence that is essential to both private deliberation and responsible citizenship in a democratic republic."

The Thinking Critically series challenges students to become discerning readers, to think independently, and to engage and develop their skills as critical thinkers. Through a narrative-driven, pro/con format, the series introduces students to the complex issues that dominate public discourse—topics such as gun control and violence, social networking, and medical marijuana. All chapters revolve around a single, pointed question such as Can Stronger Gun Control Measures Prevent Mass Shootings?, or Does Social Networking Benefit Society?, or Should Medical Marijuana Be Legalized? This inquiry-based approach introduces student researchers to core issues and concerns on a given topic. Each chapter includes one part that argues the affirmative and one part that argues the negative—all written by a single author. With the single-author format the predominant arguments for and against an issue can be synthesized into clear, accessible discussions supported by details and evidence including relevant facts, direct quotes, current examples, and statistical illustrations. All volumes include focus questions to guide students as they read each pro/con discussion, a list of key facts, and an annotated list of related organizations and websites for conducting further research.

The authors of the Common Core State Standards have set out the particular qualities that a literate person in the twenty-first century must have. These include the ability to think independently, establish a base of knowledge across a wide range of subjects, engage in open-minded but discerning reading and listening, know how to use and evaluate evidence, and appreciate and understand diverse perspectives. The new Thinking Critically series supports these goals by providing a solid introduction to the study of pro/con issues.

The Mobile Life

In January 2012, eighteen-year-old college freshman Taylor Sauer was making the four-hour drive from Utah State University to visit her family in Caldwell, Idaho. It was late at night, and as she sped along the highway, the teen used her cell phone to send text messages and message friends on Facebook. "I think she was probably (texting) to stay awake, she was probably tired," says Taylor's dad, Clay Sauer. "But that's not a reason to do it, and the kids think they're invincible. To them, (texting) is not distracting, they're so proficient at texting, that they don't feel it's distracted driving."[1] Taylor herself recognized the danger of texting while driving, and in her final message she typed, "I can't discuss this now. Driving and facebooking is not safe! Haha."[2] Moments later, Sauer's car smashed into the rear of a tanker truck that was slowly driving up a hill at about 15 miles per hour (24 km/h). Sauer was killed instantly.

An accident investigation found no evidence that Sauer, who was traveling at more than 80 miles per hour (129 km/h), applied the brakes before she hit the tanker truck—a finding that suggests she probably did not notice the truck until it was too late. When investigators checked her cell phone records, they discovered that Sauer was texting and posting about every ninety seconds as she drove, right up until the deadly crash. "The text messages were both incoming and outgoing during her trip between Logan, Utah [and the accident scene]. In addition to the texting, there were multiple Facebook communications to and from Taylor Sauer during the minutes immediately prior to the crash,"[3] says Lieutenant Sheldon Kelley of the Idaho State Police.

Sauer's family believes that Taylor's cell phone was a fatal distraction for their daughter. "We know through Taylor's Facebook account that she was actively in a conversation 12 to 15 minutes before the accident occurred. We know that Taylor had done that in the past, and we know, as a family, that that probably or may have contributed to the accident,"[4] says her uncle Brad Warr. As a result, Taylor's parents have lobbied for laws that restrict cell phone use in the hopes that they will prevent more tragedy.

Widespread Adoption

Since the first handheld cellular phone was introduced in the 1970s, cell phones have become an integral part of daily life around the world. According to an October 2012 report by the International Telecommunications Union (ITU), a United Nations agency, worldwide cell phone usage has grown tremendously in the past few years. Worldwide, people had purchased 6 billion cell phone subscriptions through the end of 2011, with approximately one-third coming from China and India. In addition, mobile broadband services, which are used by smartphones, have also grown rapidly—overtaking the fixed-broadband services needed for landlines. "Over the past year, growth in mobile-broadband services continued at 40 percent globally and 78 percent in developing countries," the ITU said in a 2012 statement. "There are now twice as many mobile-broadband subscriptions as fixed-broadband subscriptions worldwide."[5]

In the United States cell phones have exploded in popularity. About 87 percent of American adults own a cell phone, according to the Pew Internet & American Life Project. In addition, CTIA, the industry group for wireless providers in America, reported that between July 2011 and June 2012, there were more mobile phone subscriptions (322 million) than there were Americans (314 million), showing that mobile technology has grown so popular that some people have multiple phones. During that same period, CTIA reported that Americans spent about 2.3 trillion minutes on their cell phones. Text messaging also increased about 3 percent between 2011 and 2012, with Americans sending about 2.3 trillion texts.

Distracted Driving Laws by State, 2012

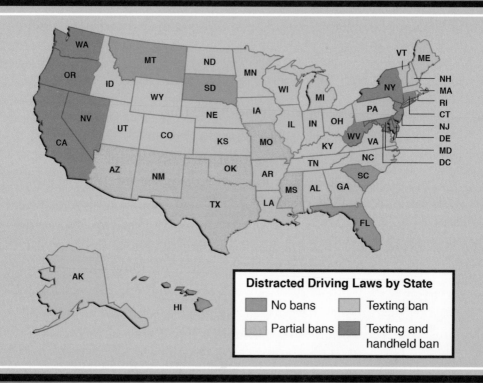

Note: Partial bans refer to states that have laws prohibiting certain groups of drivers from using a handheld device or texting behind the wheel. Often, these bans are directed toward novice or bus drivers. With the exception of Michigan, New Hampshire, and Utah, all states with a texting ban also have a partial handheld cell phone usage ban in place. New Mexico's handheld ban is for drivers with in-state vehicles and novice drivers. The District of Columbia has a texting and handheld ban.

Source: Distraction.gov, "State Laws," December 19, 2012. www.distraction.gov.

Cell Phone Use

Although early cell phones only provided limited voice services, to-day's mobile phones can be used for many functions. Whereas the simplest phones make basic voice calls, more advanced models also provide data services that allow users to send text messages and check e-mail from the palm of their hand. Smartphones operate like mini-computers, allowing users to connect to the Internet, browse websites, research questions, read documents, and bank online. In addition to being a tool for communication and information, cell phones are entertainment hubs, with users watching movies, listening to music, taking pictures and video, playing games, and reading books on their phones. Special applications can even turn a phone into a portable GPS device.

Cell phones have become an indispensable tool that many people carry with them at all times. "Cell users now treat their gadget as a body appendage," says Lee Rainie, director of the Pew Internet & American Life Project. "There is striking growth in the number of people who are taking advantage of the growing number of functions that these phones can perform and there isn't much evidence yet that the pace of change is slowing down."[6]

How Cell Phones Work

Cell phones allow people to be connected almost anywhere. Users can make calls, send texts, or surf the Internet from their cars, at the mall, or on the beach. Communication is no longer restricted by landline phones or computers. Wherever they can get a signal, cell phones work.

Cell phones operate by using a transmitter inside the phone to turn a user's voice into an electrical signal. The phone's antenna transmits the electronic signals as radio waves through the air. Because the cell phone's small antenna can only send a signal over a relatively short distance, it sends the signal to the nearest cell tower. Cell towers are part of a cellular network that allows calls to travel over long distances. The cellular network divides land into a patchwork of hexagonal areas called cells, each of which has its own cell tower or base station. The base station picks up signals from a mobile phone and relays it to the next base station. This relay repeats from tower to tower until the signal is within range of the call's destination. When the signal finally reaches the destination phone, a transmitter converts it back into a voice.

Cell Phones and Driving Laws

While cell phones are extremely convenient, they can also be a distraction for drivers. In the United States there are no federal laws that prohibit cell phone use in cars. Instead, drivers face a patchwork of local and state laws regarding cell phone use while driving.

Regulations vary by region, county, and state. Ten states have laws that ban talking on handheld cell phones while driving, although using a phone with a hands-free device is permitted. In thirty-three states novice drivers are restricted from using any cell phone, even a hands-free model. (Most states consider a novice driver to be any driver under the age of eighteen, but in some states this term simply refers to a new driver.) Text messaging is banned in thirty-nine states for all drivers, and an additional five states ban texting for novice drivers only. Within each of these states, the details of the texting bans vary. In some, it is only illegal to send texts while driving; in others, all electronic communication, including reading texts, is prohibited. A few states, such as South Carolina and South Dakota, have no ban of any kind on cell phone use while driving. In addition to state laws, many localities have their own laws about cell phone use and text messaging behind the wheel.

Health and Safety Concerns

Many people agree that cell phones provide benefits to society. They allow people to stay connected to friends and family without being tied to a landline or a bulky computer, can be used to call for help in an emergency, and can be used as minicomputers. At the same time, there is growing concern over the safety of cell phones. Cell phones have become the number-one cause of distracted driving, which can lead to accidents, injuries, and death. According to the National Safety Council, when users talk on cell phones while driving, they are four times as likely to crash. Likewise, drivers who text are eight to twenty-three times more likely to be involved in a traffic accident. Cell phones also emit radiation, which some people believe may cause a variety of health problems, from cancer to fertility issues.

While they have many useful applications, cell phones have also been associated with negative behaviors. Some teens have used cell phones for sexting and cyberbullying, practices that can cause emotional and psychological damage as well as carry legal consequences. In addition, cell phone use can become extreme for some people, and they experience anxiety and withdrawal symptoms when not connected to their phone.

Despite concerns, cell phones have been embraced by users around the world. From crowded American cities to remote African villages, cell phones connect the world and have forever changed how people communicate, do business, find information, and view entertainment. A generation ago, a cell phone was a science-fiction dream. Today it has become a necessity of life. "Just as remarkable as the power of mobility, over everything from love to learning to global development, is how fast it all happened," writes Nancy Gibbs, a best-selling author and commentator on politics and values in the United States. "It is hard to think of any tool, any instrument, any object in history with which so many developed so close a relationship so quickly as we have with our phones."[7]

Chapter One

Are Stronger Laws Needed to Prevent Cell Phone Use by Drivers?

Stronger Laws Are Needed

- States and municipalities with strong laws have fewer drivers using cell phones and fewer accidents related to cell phone use.
- Laws that allow use of hands-free phones while driving ignore studies that show these are a serious distraction.
- Drivers have no reason to take cell phone laws seriously when such laws prohibit police from stopping drivers solely because they are talking on cell phones.

The Debate at a Glance

Stronger Laws Are Not Needed

- Cell phone laws are already difficult to enforce; stronger laws will not make a difference.
- There is little evidence that cell phone bans reduce accident rates and improve road safety.
- Many people who use cell phones while driving also engage in other distracted driving practices, regardless of laws.

Stronger Laws Are Needed

"Putting restrictions in place that will reduce cell phone usage while driving helps curb distracted driving."

—Darryl M. Scott, a Delaware state representative.

Quoted in Delaware.gov, "Governor Markell Signs Legislation Restricting Drivers' Cell Phone Use," July 6, 2010. http://governor.delaware.gov.

Consider these questions as you read:

1. Taking into account the facts and ideas presented in this discussion, how persuasive is the argument that stronger laws are needed to reduce cell phone use while driving? Which arguments are strongest, and why?
2. Do you think that there is ever a reason to use a cell phone behind the wheel? Why or why not?
3. What effect, if any, would stronger laws have on driver behavior?

Editor's note: The discussion that follows presents common arguments made in support of this perspective, reinforced by facts, quotes, and examples taken from various sources.

Cell phones are a dangerous and sometimes deadly distraction that should never be used while driving. Even a momentary loss of focus while driving can lead to accident, injury, and death. According to the National Safety Council, approximately 1.1 million car crashes in the United States in 2010 involved drivers talking on their cell phones. Drivers texting on cell phones were involved in approximately 160,000 additional crashes. "Clearly these technologies have a capability of really making the crash risk go up," says David Strayer, a University of Utah psychology professor. "All you have to do is look at other drivers when they're weaving and running red lights and doing other things that are clearly hazardous and see these drivers are not drunk, they're just intoxicated with technology,"[8] Strayer says. To deter cell phone use while driving, the government should pass and enforce stronger laws that ban all cell phone use while driving.

Strong Laws Bring Results

Despite some restrictions on cell phone use while driving, many drivers ignore these laws, indicating that current laws are not strong enough to deter use. According to a December 2011 survey by the National Highway Traffic Safety Administration (NHTSA), 80 percent of males and 73 percent of females said that they would answer the phone while driving. A smaller but still significant number (43 percent of males and 39 percent of females) said that they made calls on their phones while driving. Clearly, existing laws are not having the desired effect. Stronger and more comprehensive laws are needed to get people to put phones down and improve road safety.

States with laws that prohibit the use of handheld phones while driving have seen positive results. In California a study released in 2012 by the state Office of Traffic Safety (OTS) showed that laws prohibiting drivers from using handheld phones, combined with increased enforcement efforts, can reduce driver phone use and related traffic fatalities. In 2008 California had implemented a state law that banned the use of handheld cell phones. Researchers at the Safe Transportation Research and Education Center (SafeTREC) at the University of California, Berkeley, compared state crash records two years before and after the ban was implemented. They found that vehicle accident fatalities caused by drivers using handheld cell phones decreased 47 percent after the ban went into effect. "These results suggest that the law banning hand-held cell phone use while driving had a positive impact on reducing traffic fatalities and injuries,"[9] says David Ragland, the director of SafeTREC. A separate survey conducted by the OTS in 2011 found that 40 percent of respondents reported that the ban had changed their behavior, and they were using

> "These results suggest that the law banning hand-held cell phone use while driving had a positive impact on reducing traffic fatalities and injuries."[9]
>
> —David Ragland, the director of SafeTREC.

Americans Open to Stronger Laws

Americans understand the dangers of cell phone use by drivers and are open to a ban on such use. In a 2013 report from the US Department of Transportation more than 70 percent of respondents said that handheld phone use behind the wheel was dangerous and more than 90 percent said that texting was dangerous. A smaller but still significant number of people opposed the use of hands-free phones while driving.

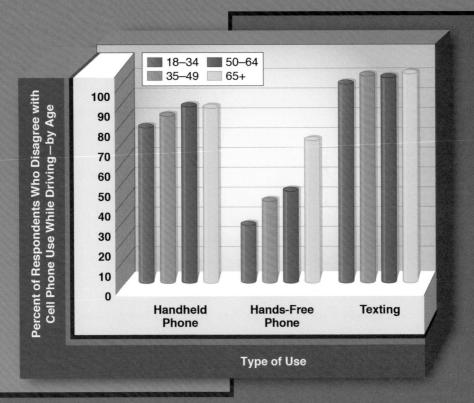

Source: Jenny Guarino, "Survey Reveals Public Is Open to Ban on Hand-Held Cell Phone Use and Texting," US Department of Transportation, January 2013. www.rita.dot.gov.

their cell phones less in the car. "The driving public understands that this is risky behavior, and most people are complying,"[10] says Jo Simitian, a state senator and the author of California's ban.

Strong laws and targeted enforcement are also working in other states. In 2011 the NHTSA reported that pilot programs in Hartford,

Connecticut, and Syracuse, New York, succeeded in reducing driver cell phone use. Both programs implemented aggressive public service campaigns to inform drivers of strong penalties for cell phone use while driving and increased enforcement efforts. In Hartford, officials reported that cell phone use and texting dropped by a third during the enforcement period. In Syracuse officials reported that handheld cell phone use dropped by more than 50 percent and texting by nearly 75 percent. "The success of these pilot programs clearly shows that combining strong laws with strong enforcement can bring about a sea change in public attitudes and behavior,"[11] says NHTSA administrator David Strickland.

One important feature of stronger laws is stronger penalties for violations. In 2013 the New Jersey legislature proposed a bill that would increase fines and license suspensions for drivers caught talking or texting on their cell phones. The bill doubles fines from $100 to $200 for the first offense, and it assesses a $400 fine for the second offense and a $600 fine (and the possibility of a driver's license suspension) for the third offense. The bill's sponsor, state senator Richard Codey, commented that current fines were not enough to stop drivers from using phones. "Right now that's a slap on the wrist, and what we've got to do is a slap on the face," Codey says. "And this bill does exactly that and hopefully wakes up the public."[12]

Hands-Free Devices Are Just as Dangerous

The strongest and best laws would ban the use of all cell phones, whether handheld or hands-free. "There is a large body of evidence showing that talking on a phone, whether hand-held or hands-free, impairs driving and increases your risk of having a crash,"[13] says Anne McCartt, the senior vice president for research at the Insurance Institute for Highway Safety.

According to researchers, when a person talks on the phone, even while using a hands-free device, the brain listens and processes what is being said rather than being focused on driving. In 2011 the National Safety Council issued a paper that reviewed more than thirty scientific studies and reports and concluded that using a cell phone requires the brain to multitask. Although people think they are multitasking when they do several things at once, the brain is actually shifting from one task to another, not performing multiple tasks simultaneously. According to David Meyer, a cognitive scientist at the University of Michigan, this shifting occurs because the brain's ability to process information is limited. When drivers use cell phones, their brains use the same processing channel for both tasks, shifting back and forth between driving and phone tasks. If a driver attempts to have a cell phone conversation while driving, Meyer says that either the conversation or the driving will suffer.

As a result, drivers using cell phones have difficulty monitoring their surroundings, seeing and identifying hazards, and responding to unexpected situations on the road. "Several states and municipalities have passed legislation allowing hands-free devices while driving," says Janet Froetscher, the National Safety Council president. "These laws give the false impression that hands-free phones are a safe alternative, when the evidence is clear they are not. Understanding the distraction of the brain will help people make the right decision and put down their cell phones while driving."[14]

> "There is a large body of evidence showing that talking on a phone, whether hand-held or hands-free, impairs driving and increases your risk of having a crash."[13]
>
> —Anne McCartt, the senior vice president for research at the Insurance Institute for Highway Safety.

Recognizing the danger posed by hands-free cell phone use, in December 2011 the National Transportation Safety Board (NTSB) called for a nationwide ban on all portable electronic devices while driving, including hands-free devices. According to NTSB chairman Deborah A.P. Hersman, the key to driving safety is where a driver's head is, not his or her hands. Under the NTSB recommendation, the only exception to the ban would be for devices such as GPS units, which are intended to support driving. "No call, no text, no update, is worth a human life," says Hersman. "It is time for all of us to stand up for safety by turning off electronic devices when driving."[15]

Cell Phone Use Should Be a Primary Offense

In many jurisdictions cell phone law violations are enforced as secondary offenses. This means that police officers can only cite drivers for using cell phones if they have another reason to stop them, such as for speeding. "You have to be doing something else before a police officer can pull you over,"[16] says Jimmy Malone, a Maryland state delegate.

For cell phone laws to be taken seriously by drivers, violations should be enforced as a primary offense. This would allow police officers to stop drivers for using their phones even if drivers are obeying all other traffic rules. As of 2012, only nine states and the District of Columbia enforced cell phone bans as primary offenses. In Maryland a bill introduced in 2012 would make using a cell phone behind the wheel a primary offense. Currently, Maryland has a no-texting law that allows police to pull drivers over for texting while driving without any other violations. "Extending that to holding phones will most likely make motorists obey the law and increase the enforceability of the current statute,"[17] says Christine Delise of the American Automobile Association (AAA) Mid-Atlantic.

Using cell phones while driving is a dangerous and potentially deadly distraction. Yet people continue to talk while driving, putting their lives and the lives of others at risk. Strong laws that ban all cell phone use and are enforced as a primary offense are key components of keeping roads safe for all travelers.

Stronger Laws Are Not Needed

"Cell phone bans have reduced cell phone use by drivers, but the perplexing thing is that they haven't reduced crashes."

—Russ Rader, a spokesperson for the Insurance Institute for Highway Safety.

Quoted in Carol Cruzan Morton, "Why Cell Phone Bans Don't Work," *Science*NOW, August 22, 2012. http://news.sciencemag.org.

Consider these questions as you read:

1. Taking into account the facts and ideas presented in this discussion, how persuasive is the argument that stronger laws are not needed to prevent cell phone use by drivers? Which arguments are strongest, and why?
2. Do you think cell phone use should be permitted in certain situations? Why or why not?
3. Are there ways other than strengthening cell phone laws to reduce distracted driving? Explain your answer.

Editor's note: The discussion that follows presents common arguments made in support of this perspective, reinforced by facts, quotes, and examples taken from various sources.

Laws that ban cell phones while driving are difficult to enforce, yield questionable results, and do not address the real problem: driver distraction. Today's drivers face many distractions behind the wheel. In addition to cell phones, drivers are distracted by eating, changing radio stations, talking to passengers, or disciplining children. Any of these distractions can lead to accidents and injuries. A study released in January 2013 by the AAA Foundation for Traffic Safety found that 90 percent of people believe distracted driving is a bigger problem than it was three years ago, but many people still engage in behaviors behind the wheel that take their attention off of their driving.

Stronger laws aimed at reducing cell phone use will have little effect on distracted driving. Adrian Lund, president of the Insurance Institute for Highway Safety in Arlington, Virginia, says that he has seen few results from restrictions on cell phone use in his state, and bans have not reduced crashes significantly. Lund believes this indicates that stronger laws against driving while using cell phones will not be effective. "Maybe if they're not talking on their cell phones, they'll be distracting themselves with something else,"[18] he says.

Bans Are Difficult to Enforce

Although legislatures can pass laws that ban cell phone use while driving, enforcement of these laws is extremely difficult for police officers. When a driver passes by, it is hard to tell the difference between one who is texting or making a phone call and one who is just glancing down or looking for something on the seat or floor of the car. "I think using a cell phone while driving is stupid," says Betty Olson, a South Dakota state representative who opposes a cell phone ban in her state. "But the last thing the cops need is another law to try to enforce."[19]

> "Maybe if they're not talking on their cell phones, they'll be distracting themselves with something else."[18]
>
> —Adrian Lund, president of the Insurance Institute for Highway Safety in Arlington, Virginia.

In states where bans exist, police officers admit the difficulty of enforcement. Many times, officers simply cannot see if drivers are using phones, especially if they are holding them in their laps. In Delaware a ban on using cell phones while driving went into effect in January 2011. Sergeant Paul Shavack with the Delaware State Police says that "it's hard to tell if the driver was using a cell phone unless he or she admits it or a witness says it's happening."[20] Texting is banned in Utah, but drivers there can legally use handheld cell phones, including searching for numbers and dialing, while behind the wheel. Utah Highway Patrol trooper Todd Johnson says that catching drivers who text is challenging. "It's difficult to do the enforcement on it because the officer or trooper or police officer needs to be certain that the person is texting and it's hard to tell,"[21] he says.

No Evidence Exists That Stronger Laws Reduce Accidents

Although some people are calling for stronger cell phone laws to reduce accident rates, there is no conclusive evidence that stronger laws make roads safer. A 2012 study led by researchers at the University of Illinois found that cell phone bans have mixed results. The researchers studied long-term accident rate trends and their link to cell phone bans. They compared seven years of driver data from New York, which had banned handheld cell phones in 2001, and Pennsylvania, which has no state ban. "Most other studies focus on a very short-term analysis," says study leader Sheldon H. Jacobson, a professor of computer science and mathematics at the University of Illinois. "We try to take a much longer view and look at the impact not just over six months to a year, but over several years."[22]

In all areas, the researchers discovered that enacting a cell phone ban had mixed results. Over time, urban areas with higher driver density experienced a decrease in auto accidents. In contrast, accident rates increased in rural areas over the same period. "What we found in our research is that the cellphone ban was associated with different outcomes in different groups of counties," says Douglas King, the study coauthor and an industrial engineering researcher. "Based on this research, it suggests that a blanket cellphone ban may not always lead to a greater benefit. Based on the seven-year time period that we were able to examine, the outcome in each group of counties after the ban was not uniformly beneficial,"[23] says King.

Other studies have found that texting bans have no effect on accident crash rates. In a 2010 study by the Insurance Institute for Highway Safety, researchers found that there was no corresponding decrease in crash risk when texting laws were enacted:

> The results of this study seem clear. In none of the four states where texting bans could be studied was there a reduction in crashes. . . . If the goal of texting and cell phone bans is the reduction of crash risk, then the bans have so far been ineffective. Bans on handheld cell phone use by drivers have had no effect on crashes, as measured by collision claim frequencies, and texting bans may actually have increased crashes.[24]

Stronger Texting Bans Do Not Reduce Collisions

Bans of texting behind the wheel aim to improve road safety and reduce crashes caused by drivers distracted by texting. Yet an analysis of insurance collision claims does not indicate a decline in crash risk when texting bans are implemented. According to a 2010 study by the Highway Loss Data Institute, collision claims in California as reported by insurance companies actually increased overall after a January 2009 texting ban for all drivers as compared with three neighboring states that either did not have a ban or only banned texting for teen drivers.

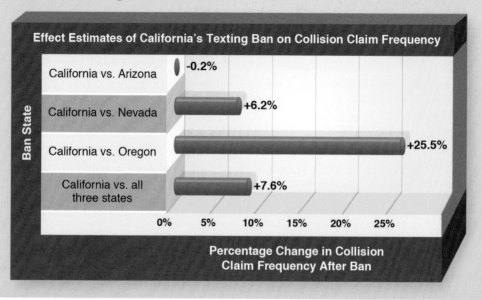

Effect Estimates of California's Texting Ban on Collision Claim Frequency

Ban State	Percentage Change
California vs. Arizona	-0.2%
California vs. Nevada	+6.2%
California vs. Oregon	+25.5%
California vs. all three states	+7.6%

Percentage Change in Collision Claim Frequency After Ban

Source: *Highway Loss Data Institute Bulletin,* "Texting Laws and Collision Claim Frequency," September 2010.

The authors also say that the increase in crashes in states with texting bans may result from people trying to hide their texting behavior to avoid fines—an action that actually causes them to take their eyes off the road.

High-Risk Drivers Cause Accidents

Some research has found that certain people are more likely to engage in high-risk, distracted behavior while driving, regardless of laws. A 2013

AAA Foundation for Traffic Safety study found that drivers who regularly talk on cell phones behind the wheel also were likely to speed (65 percent), drive while drowsy (44 percent), or drive without a seatbelt (29 percent). In contrast, drivers who reported that they never used a cell phone while driving were significantly more likely to obey speed limits, not drive while drowsy, and wear a seatbelt. "What concerns AAA is this pattern of risky behavior that even goes beyond cell phone use," says Kathleen Bower of AAA. "These same cell phone–using drivers clearly understand the risk of distraction, yet are still likely to engage in a wide range of dangerous driving activities."[25]

In another study, researchers from the Massachusetts Institute of Technology (MIT) found that people who talk on cell phones while driving often drive more aggressively, even when they are not on the phone. "The people who are more willing to frequently engage in cell phone use are higher-risk drivers, independent of the phone," says Bryan Reimer, the associate director of MIT's New England University Transportation Center. "It's not just a subtle difference with those willing to pick up the phone. This is a big difference."[26]

The MIT researchers studied the behavior of 108 drivers in the Boston area. Those who said they used their phones frequently in the car tended to drive faster, change lanes more often, and travel more often in the far-left lane than drivers who seldom used their phones. In addition, the frequent callers were more likely to quickly accelerate and slam on their brakes. Reimer says that the study suggests that frequent calling is one sign that a driver has a high-risk personality and is willing to engage in a variety of risky driving behaviors. "Legislating the technology alone is not going to solve our problem," says Reimer. "We need to look more at the behavior of the individual."[27]

> "I think using a cell phone while driving is stupid. But the last thing the cops need is another law to try to enforce."[19]
>
> —Betty Olson, a South Dakota state representative who opposes a cell phone ban in her state.

Enforce Existing Laws

Although most people agree that using cell phones while driving increases the likelihood of accidents and injuries, little evidence exists that stronger laws restricting cell phone use will have a significant effect on driver behavior or improve road safety. Instead, efforts to better enforce existing distracted-driving laws and provide education about the risks of driving while distracted are more likely to motivate drivers to disconnect from their phones. "More work clearly is needed to educate motorists on the risks associated with using a cell phone while driving, especially given that most Americans believe this problem is becoming worse,"[28] says Peter Kissinger, the president of the AAA Foundation for Traffic Safety.

Chapter Two

Do Cell Phones Pose a Health Hazard?

Cell Phones Are a Health Hazard

- Cell phone radiation has been linked to changes in the brain, some of which might lead to cancer.
- Researchers have identified cell phone radiation as a possible cause of male infertility.
- Damage from cell phone radiation may be a possible cause of brain changes that have been linked to ADHD.

The Debate at a Glance

Cell Phones Are Not a Health Hazard

- Cell phones emit nonionizing radiation; this type of radiation does not affect human health.
- Most scientific research into possible links between cell phone radiation and cancer has found no such correlation.
- Although cell phone use might trigger some brain activity, scientists have found no harm to the brain from this activity.

Cell Phones Are a Health Hazard

"I think it is a good idea to give the public some sort of warning that long-term exposure to radiation from your cell phone could possibly cause cancer."

—Henry Lai, a research professor in bioengineering at the University of Washington.

Quoted in Danielle Dellorto, "WHO: Cell Phone Use Can Increase Possible Cancer Risk," CNN.com, May 31, 2011. www.cnn.com.

Consider these questions as you read:

1. How persuasive is the argument that cell phones are a health hazard? Which arguments are strongest, and why?
2. Do you think the public is adequately informed about the possible health effects of cell phone use? Why or why not?
3. Do you think this argument will change how you use cell phones? Why or why not?

Editor's note: The discussion that follows presents common arguments made in support of this perspective, reinforced by facts, quotes, and examples taken from various sources.

Global cell phone use has exploded. According to the International Telecommunications Union, the world has almost 5 billion cell phone users, and people are making more calls and longer calls than ever before. With the rise of cell phones, new worries have surfaced about possible health hazards. Cell phones emit radiation, which has been linked to cancer, fertility problems, behavioral problems, and other health issues. Dr. Keith Black, the chairman of neurology at Cedars-Sinai Medical Center in Los Angeles, says concern about cell phone radiation is warranted. He compares the radiation from cell phones to that emitted by low-powered microwave ovens. "What microwave radiation does in most simplistic terms is similar to what happens to food in microwaves, essentially cooking the brain," says Black. "So in addition to leading to a development of cancer and tumors, there could be a whole host of other effects."[29]

Cell Phone Radiation Is Linked to Cancer

Cell phones emit radio waves, which are a form of electromagnetic radiation. Tissue near where the phone is held by the ear can absorb this energy, which has been linked to certain types of cancer. In 2011 the World Health Organization warned that radiation from cell phones could cause cancer and listed mobile phones as a carcinogenic hazard, similar to lead, engine exhaust, and chloroform. Before issuing the warning, a team of thirty-one scientists from fourteen countries reviewed numerous studies on cell phone safety. The team found evidence of an increase in certain brain cancers—specifically glioma and acoustic neuroma—in mobile phone users. In 2010 the Interphone study, a thirteen-country international study on cell phones and cancer, reported that participants who used a cell phone for ten years or longer had a 40 percent higher rate of brain gliomas. "To me, there's certainly smoke there," says Elisabeth Cardis, the project leader and a researcher with the Center for Research in Environment Epidemiology in Barcelona, Spain. "Overall, my opinion is that the results show a real effect."[30]

The risk of cancer may be even higher for young cell phone users. Although long-term studies on the effects of cell phone radiation on children and teens have not been done, scientists know that the developing brain of a young person is more susceptible than the adult brain to environmental influences. This suggests that a young person's brain might be more susceptible to cell phone radiation. "Children's skulls and scalps are thinner. So the radiation can penetrate deeper into the brain of children and young adults. Their cells are dividing at a faster rate, so the impact of radiation can be much larger,"[31] says Black of Cedars-Sinai Medical Center.

> "Children's skulls and scalps are thinner. So the radiation can penetrate deeper into the brain of children and young adults. Their cells are dividing at a faster rate, so the impact of radiation can be much larger."[31]
>
> —Keith Black, the chairman of neurology at Cedars-Sinai Medical Center.

Cell Phones Affect Fertility

In addition to the possible link to cancer, cell phone radiation has been associated with damage to male fertility. In 2012 the Environmental Working Group, a health advocacy group, released a report on the harmful effects of cell phones on male sperm. The group reported that ten studies have found significant changes in sperm when it was exposed to cell phone radiation. The effects included DNA damage and changes in sperm form and structure, which made the sperm less likely to fertilize an egg during reproduction. "In the most striking findings, men who carried their phones in a pocket or on the belt were more likely to have lower sperm counts and/ or more inactive or less mobile sperm,"[32] the study's authors wrote.

The study also reported that men who talked on the phone for more than an hour a day had 17 percent fewer highly mobile sperm than men who talked less than fifteen minutes a day. "We have enough evidence to issue precautionary health warnings," says Joel Moskowitz, the director of the Center for Family and Community Health in the School of Public Health at the University of California, Berkeley. "The evidence for sperm damage is quite consistent across many studies,"[33] he says.

Use of hands-free devices might actually present a greater danger to male fertility than holding the phone to one's ear. The report noted that men who used a Bluetooth or other hands-free headset had lower sperm counts and less mobile sperm than men who held their phones to their ears. Researchers suspect this occurred because men using hands-free headsets usually keep their phones in their pockets or attached to a belt, close to sex organs, so sperm are constantly exposed to harmful radiation.

Cell Phones Are Linked to Behavioral Problems

The radiation from cell phones might also affect brain development. Scientists know that a pregnant woman who undergoes an X-ray or who drinks alcohol, smokes, or does drugs might harm the developing fetus. Cell phone radiation might also cause harm, such as bringing about changes in the area of the brain that controls behavior.

In 2012 researchers from the Yale School of Medicine reported that exposing pregnant mice to cell phone radiation affected the behavior of

Cell Phones Damage Sperm, Male Fertility

The radiation emitted by cell phones can damage male sperm and decrease male fertility. According to a 2012 report from the Environmental Working Group, several research studies have found that men who used their phones more frequently and carried them on or near their hips were more likely to have lower sperm counts and more inactive, less highly mobile sperm.

Study Findings Include:

Men who carried a phone in a hip pocket or on the belt had 11 percent fewer mobile sperm than men who kept a phone elsewhere on the body.

Men who carried a phone on the belt and used it intensively during a five-day test period had a 19 percent drop in highly mobile sperm from their previous levels.

Men who talked on the phone for more than an hour a day had 17 percent fewer highly mobile sperm than men who talked fewer than fifteen minutes a day.

Source: Environmental Working Group, "EWG's Guide to Safer Cell Phone Use: Cell Phone Radiation Damages Sperm, Studies Find," June 15, 2012. www.ewg.org.

their offspring. Researchers studied two groups of pregnant mice. The first group was placed in cages with active phones taped to the sides, and the second group was placed in cages with deactivated phones. The pregnant mice in the first group and their fetuses were exposed to cell phone radiation constantly until they gave birth. The other group had no exposure.

Once the mice gave birth, the researchers evaluated the offspring of both groups. The offspring mice exposed to cell phone radiation while in the womb showed signs of hyperactivity, anxiety, and memory problems; the other group did not. The researchers also examined and measured the electrical activity in the brains of mice from both groups and examined tissue samples from their prefrontal cortexes. In both mice and humans, the prefrontal cortex controls attention. The researchers found slight differences between the two groups, specifically in electrical activity in the brain. They suspect that cell phone radiation may have altered the structure of the brain cells, which might explain the observed behavioral differences. The researchers also noted that the radiation effects continued long after the mice had been separated from the phones. "This is the first experimental evidence that fetal exposure to radiofrequency radiation from cellular telephones does in fact affect adult behavior,"[34] says the study's senior author, Hugh S. Taylor, a professor and the chief of the Division of Reproductive Endocrinology and Infertility in the Department of Obstetrics, Gynecology, and Reproductive Sciences at Yale University.

The behaviors observed in the mice—hyperactivity, anxiety, and poorer memory—are symptoms associated with attention-deficit/hyperactivity disorder (ADHD), a developmental disorder. In the United States the number of children diagnosed with ADHD has risen 66 percent between 2000 and 2010, according to a study published in 2012 in the journal *Academic Pediatrics*. The Yale researchers warn that cell phones might be one factor in the rise in ADHD in children. "We have shown that behavioral problems in mice that resemble ADHD are caused by cell phone exposure in the womb," says Taylor. "The rise in behavioral disorders in human children may be in part due to fetal cellular telephone irradiation exposure."[35]

> "The rise in behavioral disorders in human children may be in part due to fetal cellular telephone irradiation exposure."[35]
>
> —Hugh S. Taylor, a professor and the chief of the Division of Reproductive Endocrinology at Yale University.

As more people rely on cell phones, the health risks associated with cell phones and the radiation they emit cannot be ignored. More research is needed to better understand the variety of ways in which these devices impact health. With this knowledge, users can make informed decisions about whether to limit their cell phone use in order to protect their bodies and brains.

Cell Phones Are Not a Health Hazard

"The weight of scientific evidence has not linked cell phones with any health problems."

—US Food and Drug Administration

US Food and Drug Administration, "Health Issues: Do Cell Phones Pose a Health Hazard?," FDA.gov, August 8, 2012. www.fda.gov.

Consider these questions as you read:

1. Taking into account the facts and ideas presented in this discussion, how persuasive is the argument that cell phones are not a health hazard? Which arguments are strongest, and why?
2. Do you believe that changes in brain activity caused by cell phone use are harmless? Why or why not?
3. Do you think that there has been enough time to study the long-term effects of cell phones on health? Why or why not?

Editor's note: The discussion that follows presents common arguments made in support of this perspective, reinforced by facts, quotes, and examples taken from various sources.

Cell phone radiation has been blamed for health concerns ranging from brain cancer to behavioral problems to male fertility issues. So far, however, there is no consistent scientific evidence to support the view that cell phones are a health hazard. Mobile phones have been around for decades, yet there is no evidence of a significant increase in brain tumors or other related health problems, says Paul Graham Fisher, a professor of neurology at Stanford University School of Medicine. "It's not an unreasonable concern," he says. "But right now there really isn't any evidence to say it's a problem."[36]

Concerns over Cell Phone Radiation Are Overblown

Concerns about radiation from cell phones causing a variety of health problems are greatly exaggerated. Cell phones emit radio frequency (RF) fields, which are low-level electromagnetic fields produced when a mobile phone or other wireless device uses an antenna to send and receive radio signals. The RF energy emitted by cell phones is a form of electromagnetic radiation—that is, waves of electric and magnetic energy that radiate through space.

Electromagnetic radiation can be classified into two types. Ionizing radiation, which has been linked to health problems and an increased risk of cancer, is found in X-rays and gamma rays. Ionizing radiation is strong enough to cause molecular changes in the objects it contacts. Cell phones emit nonionizing radiation. Nonionizing radiation is weaker and has a longer wavelength than ionizing radiation. It does not change the structure of the atoms it contacts. Other examples of nonionizing radiation include radio waves, microwaves, visible light, and infrared light. Although many studies have investigated the health effects of nonionizing radiation, there is no consistent scientific evidence that nonionizing radiation increases cancer risk or causes other health problems.

This conclusion is supported by many public health and governmental agencies, including the National Institute of Environmental Health Sciences, the US Food and Drug Administration, the Federal Communications Commission (FCC), and the Centers for Disease Control and Prevention (CDC). According to the FCC's website:

> In recent years, publicity, speculation, and concern over claims of possible health effects due to RF emissions from hand-held wireless telephones prompted various research programs to investigate whether there is any risk to users of these devices. There is no scientific evidence to date that proves that wireless phone usage can lead to cancer or a variety of other health effects, including headaches, dizziness or memory loss.[37]

In 2012 the Norwegian Institute of Public Health released a two-hundred-page study on the health risks of exposure to the low-level electromagnetic fields that can be found near mobile (or cell) phones, wireless phones (such as landlines found in many homes) and networks, mobile phone base stations, and broadcasting transmitters. The study found no health risks associated with mobile phones or other electronics that wirelessly transmit signals. The institute concluded, "There is no evidence to support the belief that low-level electromagnetic field exposure from electronics, mobile phones and wireless networks are detrimental to health, including the risk of cancer."[38]

Cell Phones Do Not Cause Cancer

Fears that radiation from cell phones might cause brain tumors or other types of cancers are also unfounded. Most cancers develop when an organism's DNA is damaged, which allows cancerous cells to form and multiply. Yet the type of radiation that cell phones emit—RF energy—does not damage DNA in cells.

Many studies have looked at the effects of RF energy on cells, animals, and humans, yet there is no conclusive evidence linking RF energy to cancer. The World Health Organization's International Agency for Research on Cancer (IARC) coordinated the largest international study of mobile phone safety, known as the European Interphone study. In the study, researchers in thirteen countries analyzed the use of mobile phones and the risk of head and neck tumors. The study's results were released in 2010 with analyses showing no statistically significant increase in brain or central nervous system cancers as a result of higher cell phone use. The researchers concluded that there was no link between cell phone use and certain brain tumors—specifically glioma and meningioma—and that mobile phones do not raise the risk of brain cancer, except for a possible slight increase in tumors for the heaviest users. "This research has not shown evidence of an increased risk of developing a glioma or meningioma brain tumour as a result of using a mobile [phone],"[39] says Patricia McKinney,

> "There is no scientific evidence to date that proves that wireless phone usage can lead to cancer or a variety of other health effects, including headaches, dizziness or memory loss."[37]
>
> —Federal Communications Commission, a government agency that monitors communication by radio, television, wire, satellite, and cable.

Brain Cancer Diagnoses Fall as Cell Phone Use Increases

The fear of cell phone radiation causing brain cancers is exaggerated and unfounded. If cell phone radiation caused cancer, the number of cancer cases should have increased along with cell phone use. Instead, the opposite has occurred. The number of Americans diagnosed with brain cancer has dropped since 1991, while cell phone use dramatically increased over the same period.

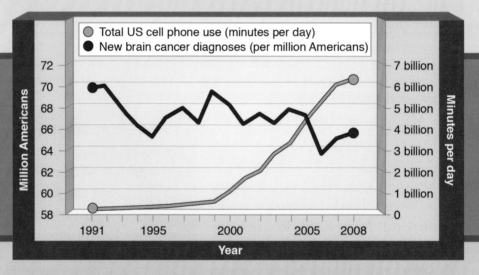

Source: CNNMoney.com, "Cell Phone Use Is Way Up. So Why Did Brain Cancer Rates Fall?," June 7, 2011.
http://tech.fortune.cnn.com.

an epidemiologist at Leeds University who led the northern UK part of the study.

Other studies have come to similar conclusions. A study described in the journal *Bioelectromagnetics* in 2011 investigated the number of cases of brain cancer in the United Kingdom between 1998 and 2007. During this period cell phone use increased dramatically. The researchers predicted that if cell phones cause brain cancer, they would expect to find that the number of cases of brain cancer would also increase during the same period at a similar rate. Yet investigators found that the number of cases of brain cancer did not increase. And in 2012 a two-hundred-page study by the Norwegian Institute of Public Health also found no scientific evidence that cell phones led to an increased risk of developing head and neck cancers. Orv Swenson, an associate professor of physics at North Dakota State University, says that the fears about cell phones and cancer are overblown. "These have been around for a long time and I don't think there's any cause for cancer," he says about mobile phones. "[There is] a lot more risk from having a traffic accident because you're using it than a long-term cancer effect."[40]

Research Finds No Harm to the Brain

While the link between cell phone radiation and cancer remains unproven, talking on a cell phone might trigger some harmless brain activity. In a study published in the *Journal of the American Medical Association* in 2012, researchers used positron-emission tomography scans to look at the brains of forty-seven people while they made fifty-minute cell phone calls. The researchers found that the parts of the brain nearest to the cell phone's antenna were about 7 percent more active when the study subjects were on the phone receiving a call than when they were not on the phone. According to Nora Volkow, the head of the National Institute on Drug Abuse and a lead author of the study, the increase in brain activity observed in the study is approximately the same amount of activity seen in the language areas of the brain during speech. "Results of this study provide evidence that acute cell phone exposure affects brain metabolic activity. However, these results provide no information as to their relevance regarding potential carcinogenic effects (or lack of such effects) from chronic cell phone use,"[41] wrote the study's authors.

> "There is no evidence to support the belief that low-level electromagnetic field exposure from electronics, mobile phones and wireless networks are detrimental to health, including the risk of cancer."[38]
>
> —Norwegian Institute of Public Health, a government agency that monitors the health of the country's population and focuses on health promotion and disease prevention.

Concerns about cell phone use as a potential health hazard have been exaggerated. To date, there is no conclusive evidence that cell phones pose risks to human health.

Chapter Three

How Do Cell Phones Impact Teens?

Concerns About Teen Cell Phone Use Are Justified

- Cell phones are a dangerous distraction for teen drivers.
- Teen health and well-being are seriously threatened by sexting and bullying via cell phones.
- Cell phones are a distraction for teens in social situations and at school.

The Debate at a Glance

Concerns About Teen Cell Phone Use Are Overblown

- Reports of sexting and cyberbullying by teens are exaggerated.
- Teens are using cell phones for communication, research, and other legitimate needs.
- For teens without other Internet access, cell phones have become a way to bridge the digital divide.

Concerns About Teen Cell Phone Use Are Justified

"It's especially risky for young, inexperienced drivers—who are already extremely vulnerable to crashes—to be distracted when they are behind the wheel. Answering a call or reading a text is never worth a loss of life."

—Linda C. Degutis, the director of the CDC's National Center for Injury Prevention and Control.

Quoted in Centers for Disease Control and Prevention, "Mobile Device Use While Driving More Common in the US than in Several European Countries," press release, March 14, 2013. www.cdc.gov.

Consider these questions as you read:

1. How persuasive is the argument that concerns about teen cell phone use are justified? Which arguments are strongest, and why?
2. Do you agree with the perspective that concerns about teen cell phone use are justified? Why or why not?
3. What do you think should be done to address concerns about teen cell phone use? Why?

Editor's note: The discussion that follows presents common arguments made in support of this perspective, reinforced by facts, quotes, and examples taken from various sources.

Cell phones have become an indispensable part of teen life. According to the Pew Internet & American Life Project, more than 75 percent of American teens have cell phones. More than just a way to call or text, teens are increasingly using phones to play games, take pictures, share videos, listen to music, and access the Internet.

Unfortunately, many teens have allowed their cell phones to practically take over their lives. Cell phone use has become a distraction in school and in social settings. The novelty of connecting to friends and others at all times of day and night has also clouded the judgment of many teens. Sexting (sending sexually explicit photos, texts, or messages by cell phone) and cyberbullying have become serious problems. Likewise, teens who drive while texting or reading messages on their phones represent a new and deadly hazard—both for themselves and others.

Cell Phones Distract Teen Drivers

Although there have always been distractions for teen drivers, cell phones have become one of the most common causes of teen distracted driving. In the National Youth Risk Behavior Survey released in 2012, the CDC reported that 58 percent of high school seniors and 43 percent of high school juniors said that they had texted or e-mailed while driving during the previous month. "A lot of teens say 'Well, if the car's not moving and I'm at a stoplight or I'm stuck in traffic, that's OK,'"[42] says Amanda Lenhart, a senior researcher at the Pew Research Center in Washington, DC, who studies how teens use technology. Other teens admit that although they know texting and driving is not safe, they think it is safer if they hold the phone up so they can see the road and the phone's screen at the same time.

When teen drivers are distracted by cell phones, they are more likely to be involved in an accident. Focusing on a cell phone can lead to delayed reaction times, swerving across lanes, and other driving mistakes. According to the National Safety Council, cell phone use and texting is the cause of 25 percent of all traffic accidents. As a result, thirty-nine states have banned texting for all drivers. Five additional states have banned texting for teen drivers. "We need to teach kids, who are the most vulnerable drivers, that texting and driving don't mix,"[43] says Ray LaHood, the US transportation secretary.

> "We need to teach kids, who are the most vulnerable drivers, that texting and driving don't mix."[43]
>
> —Ray LaHood, the US transportation secretary.

When teens mix cell phones and driving, the results can be tragic. In February 2011 teen Aaron Deveau was texting while driving in Haverhill, Massachusetts. His car crossed the center line and hit another vehicle

Negative Effects of Cell Phone Use on Teens

Although teens love their phones many have experienced the negative effects of using them. According to a survey by the Pew Internet & American Life Project, more than half of teens experienced at least one negative aspect of owning a cell phone, with unwanted text messages and distracted driving being the most frequently reported concerns.

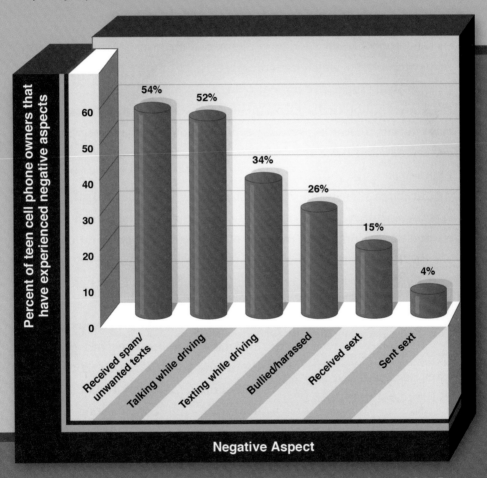

Note: Items about driving reflect teens ages 16 to 17, all other indicators are for ages 12 to 17.

Source: Pew Internet & American Life Project, "Adverse Side Effects of Teen Cell Phone Use," *Teens and Mobile Phones*, April 20, 2010. www.pewinternet.org.

traveling in the opposite direction, killing the driver and seriously injuring a passenger. In 2012 Deveau was convicted on charges of vehicular homicide, texting while driving, and negligent operation of a motor vehicle. He received a two-and-a-half-year prison sentence but was ordered to serve one year behind bars with the rest suspended. He will also serve three years of probation and lose his driver's license for fifteen years.

Cell Phones Encourage Teen Sexting

As cell phones can take and send pictures, some teens are using the technology for sexting, which is sending, receiving, or forwarding sexual photos or sexually suggestive texts or e-mails. According to a 2012 survey by the University of Utah's Department of Psychology, nearly one in five teens admits to sending sexually explicit photos or messages with their cell phones, and twice as many reported receiving sexting messages and photos.

Although some people believe that sexting is harmless, mental health experts warn that sexting can lead to emotional problems such as anxiety and depression. Many teens do not realize that photos and messages can easily land in the wrong hands. According to the University of Utah researchers, 25 percent of teens admitted to forwarding such photos or messages to someone else. "Emotionally sexting can take a toll on a person, especially if it backfires and gets into the wrong hands," says Raychelle Cassada Lohmann, a professional school counselor. "Another emotional catch is that sexting may lead to bullying for the teen whose photos have been solicited to others. This creates a harsh world for a teen to live [in]."[44]

> "Emotionally sexting can take a toll on a person, especially if it backfires and gets into the wrong hands."[44]
>
> —Raychelle Cassada Lohmann, a professional school counselor.

Teens that sext are also more likely to engage in sexual activity. The journal *Pediatrics* published a 2012 study of more than eighteen hundred Los Angeles high school students. The study found that teens who reported sexting were seven times more likely to report being sexually active. "This study is the first to show what teens are doing with their cell phones and what they're doing with their bodies,"[45] says Eric Rice, an assistant professor at the University of Southern California's School of Social Work and the study's lead author.

Teens are often unaware that sexting can have serious legal consequences. In 2012 a teen in Colorado used his cell phone to take a video of two friends engaged in a sexual act. He sent the video to another teen, who then forwarded it to others. Both teens were arrested and charged with third-degree felonies for making, possessing, and sharing the video with others. If convicted, they face a maximum sentence of two years in a juvenile detention center and would have to register as sex offenders. "There is nothing dumber than engaging in sexting behavior. It doesn't make you more attractive to the other gender and it can land you in big, big trouble,"[46] says legal analyst Scott Robinson.

Cell Phones Encourage Cyberbullying

Although teen bullying is not a new problem, cell phones enable teens to take bullying online. Cyberbullying occurs when teens use the Internet, cell phones, or other electronic devices to send or post texts or images in order to hurt or embarrass another person. Teens may use cell phones to send humiliating texts, forward embarrassing and private photos, or leave threatening messages. According to the National Crime Prevention Association, cyberbullying is a widespread problem that affects almost half of all American teens.

According to many experts, cyberbullying can be more intense and emotionally damaging than traditional bullying. When an embarrassing photo is forwarded on a phone, it can reach hundreds of peers in a very short period. In addition, the bullying can follow the teens wherever they go, as their phones receive bullying messages on the bus, at home, and on vacation. According to a 2012 report of the Nova Scotia Task Force on Bullying and Cyber-bullying, cell phones and other electronic technology have led to an increase in teen bullying. "The immediacy and broad reach of modern electronic technology has made bullying easier, faster, more prevalent and crueler than ever before,"[47] the task force reports.

Cell Phones Are a Negative Distraction

Teen sexting, cyberbullying, and even texting while driving are all part of the same problem: the inability to maintain a balance between appropriate and inappropriate uses of technology. Absent this balance, today's teens are beginning to demonstrate a reduction in the quantity and quality of face-to-face communication. Nini Halkett, a teacher at Harvard-Westlake High School in Los Angeles, says that she has noticed her students becoming increasingly distracted by cell phones and more shy and awkward in person. "They can get up the courage to ask you for [a deadline] extension on the computer," she says. "But they won't come and speak to you face-to-face about it. And that worries me, in terms of their ability—particularly once they get out in the workplace—to interact with people."[48]

In school, cell phones are a distraction from learning. With small phone screens, students are easily able to hide what they are doing from teachers. In 2012 a study conducted by researchers at the University of Haifa in Israel reported that 95 percent of high school students surveyed admitted that they regularly sent e-mails or texts from their phones during class time. In addition, 94 percent said they browsed file-sharing sites or social media sites during class, 93 percent listened to music, and 91 percent said they talked on their phones during class. "Based on our findings, there is almost no moment during any class when some pupil isn't using their cell phone,"[49] say the study's researchers.

As more teens use cell phones, there are serious concerns about the impact they have on youth. While cell phones may be useful in certain situations, their negative effects on teens may outweigh any potential benefits.

Concerns About Teen Cell Phone Use Are Overblown

"It's not really a phone, it's their computer for class. It has not taken the place of anything. It's a resource the kids can use like a book or a notebook."

—Ronald Royster, a social studies teacher whose students use cell phones to help with classwork.

Quoted in Deborah Feyerick, "School Gives Kids Cell Phones as a Teaching Tool," *American Morning* (blog), April 21, 2010. http://am.blogs.cnn.com.

Consider these questions as you read:

1. Taking into account the facts and ideas presented in this discussion, how persuasive is the argument that concerns over teen cell phone use are exaggerated? Which arguments are strongest, and why?
2. Do you agree with the perspective that teens use cell phones in creative and productive ways? Why or why not?
3. Do you think cell phones should be allowed in school? Why or why not?

Editor's note: The discussion that follows presents common arguments made in support of this perspective, reinforced by facts, quotes, and examples taken from various sources.

Concerns about how teens use cell phones have been exaggerated. For today's teens, cell phones are indispensable tools for communication, entertainment, and Internet access. For less affluent teens, cell phones have become an efficient way to access the Internet and participate in today's online society.

Exaggerated Concerns

Bad things can happen to teens anywhere, at any time. A sudden winter storm can cause a teen driver to slide and crash on a slippery road. High school bullies target teens every day for humiliation and embarrassment.

Cell Phone Bullying Less Common than In-Person

A 2011 survey finds that one in five teens were bullied within the prior year but the primary means of bullying was in face-to-face interaction. According to the survey 12 percent said they had been bullied while only 9 percent reported being bullied by text message.

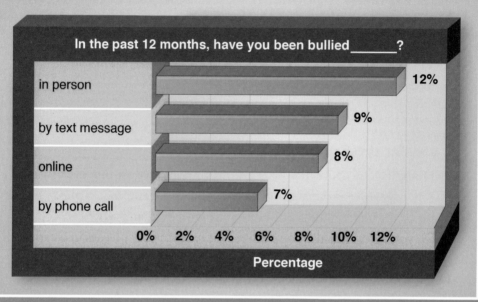

In the past 12 months, have you been bullied_____?

	Percentage
in person	12%
by text message	9%
online	8%
by phone call	7%

Source: Larry Magid, "Online Bullying: Still Way Less Common than in Real Life," CNET, November 9, 2011. http://news.cnet.com.

In school, teens have daydreamed for generations, missing out on learning and lectures. All of these things happened before teens had cell phones, and they will continue regardless of whether a teen carries a phone.

Recent studies suggest that teen sexting and cyberbullying are not as widespread as some would have people believe. Dan Olweus, a professor of psychology at Norway's University of Bergen, created one of the world's most successful school bullying prevention programs. Olweus believes that the cyberbullying threat has been exaggerated, taking the focus away from the real problem—traditional bullying. He says that there is no evidence that cyberbullying has increased in recent years, even though teen use of the Internet and mobile phones has increased. Olweus says that studies from the United States and Norway show that cyberbullying rates are one-fourth to one-third lower than traditional bullying rates. In addition, studies show that most of the victims of electronic bullying are also bullied verbally, supporting Olweus's claim that cyberbullying is not a separate problem caused by cell phones but rather an extension of traditional bullying. "These results suggest that the new electronic media have actually created few 'new' victims and bullies,"[50] says Olweus.

Other research suggests that teen sexting may not be as big a problem as originally feared. A national telephone survey conducted by researchers at the University of New Hampshire's Crimes Against Children Research Center (CACRC) surveyed 1,540 children and teens between the ages of ten and seventeen. Only 2.5 percent of the respondents said that they had appeared in or created sexually explicit images, and only 1 percent reported that they were involved in sending or receiving images that could have been considered a violation of child pornography laws. Fewer than 10 percent of respondents reported that they had sent or received sexually suggestive photos or messages.

A separate national survey of police officials found that few teens were being prosecuted under sex-offender laws for sexting unless they were also breaking other laws. Janis Wolak of the CACRC says the results show that teen sexting concerns are exaggerated. "I think parents should be reassured by this," she says. "We need to give kids credit for generally being responsible about using the Internet and navigating the other technology in their lives."[51]

> "We need to give kids credit for generally being responsible about using the Internet and navigating the other technology in their lives."[51]
>
> —Janis Wolak of the University of New Hampshire's Crimes Against Children Research Center.

In addition, some experts say that sexting is simply a natural extension of a teen's experimenting with his or her sexuality. "When we reach adolescence, we are hardwired to become sexually aware and engage in sexual behavior," says Karen North, the director of the Annenberg Program on Online Communities at the University of Southern

California. Past generations of teens may have played strip poker or looked at pornographic magazines with friends. Because today's teens have incorporated technology into almost every aspect of their daily lives, it is not surprising that they are using technology as they explore sexuality. "That behavior, which is completely normal for adolescents who are coming of age, is now being facilitated today by technology,"[52] she says.

Teens Use Cell Phones in Useful and Productive Ways

Many teens use cell phones in productive and creative ways. Cell phones have become irreplaceable communication tools for teens. Texting has become the most popular way to communicate with family and friends, with cell phone calling a close second. According to a 2012 report by the Pew Internet & American Life Project, 77 percent of teens text, with the median teen texter sending sixty texts per day. Sixty-three percent of teens say that they exchange text messages with family and friends daily, which far surpasses other forms of communication, including calling by cell phone, landline telephones, face-to-face socializing, social network messaging, e-mail, and instant messaging. Despite all the time teens spend on cell phones, some experts say that parents should not be overly concerned. Scott W. Campbell, a University of Michigan professor, says that research shows that cell phone use does not reduce the quantity of face-to-face communication. "It's an added layer of communication,"[53] says Campbell.

Teens also use cell phones as an entertainment hub. "This device has become a communication and often entertainment hub in their lives," says Pew senior researcher Amanda Lenhart. Teens use their phones to take pictures, record video, play games, listen to music, and surf the Internet. "It has become a tool to help them make sense and process and record their lives,"[54] she says. Eighteen-year-old Kyle Smith from Sandy Spring, Maryland, has owned a cell phone since he was twelve years old and says that it is a critical part of his daily life. Smith says that he uses his phone to call, text, send e-mail, take photos and video, and check the time. "I don't know what I'd do without it,"[55] he says.

A Lifeline In and Out of Class

As cell phone technology becomes more advanced, some schools are trying to incorporate phones into the classroom. Teachers at New Jersey's New Milford High School allow students to use their cell phones in class. They say that apps can turn the phones into tools such as calculators, cameras, and video cameras. Students can also use Internet tools for quick research for classroom projects and discussions. "We live in a world where these devices are a huge part of our students' lives. Schools should position themselves to not only take advantage of this resource as budgets are tight, but also teach students about the powerful tool they possess,"[56] says Eric Sheninger, New Milford High School's principal.

In addition, cell phones are an emergency line that teens can use to call parents or others for help. Many parents initially purchase a phone for their teen for safety reasons. According to a 2010 Pew study, 98 percent of parents of teens that own cell phones say that a major reason their teen has the phone is so that they can keep in touch no matter where the teen is. In addition, 94 percent of parents and 93 percent of teens ages twelve to seventeen who have cell phones agree that they feel safer having a phone.

> "Groups that have traditionally been on the other side of the digital divide in basic internet access are using wireless connections to go online."[57]
>
> —Pew Internet & American Life Project, a nonprofit, nonpartisan research organization.

Cell Phones Bridge the Digital Divide

As society increasingly connects online, there are still differences in Internet access depending on a teen's community, ethnic background, and household earnings. According to a 2012 Pew study, people living in households earning less than $30,000 per year are the least likely to have Internet access. According to the advocacy group Common Sense Media, about 48 percent of low-income families have a home computer as compared with 91 percent of higher-income families.

For teens in these lower-income households who may not have access to the Internet at home, cell phones have become a way to bridge the digital divide. As cell phone technology has improved, teens can use their phones to go online, search job listings, research school projects, and e-mail. According to Pew researchers:

Groups that have traditionally been on the other side of the digital divide in basic internet access are using wireless connections to go online. Among smartphone owners, young adults, minorities, those with no college experience, and those with lower household income levels are more likely than other groups to say that their phone is their main source of internet access.[57]

In a 2010 report, Pew researchers found that teens from low-income households were more likely to use their phones to go online than other teens. Campbell, who has studied teen cell phone use at the University of Michigan, agrees: "It does offer an opportunity some would not otherwise have."[58]

When misused, all technology can have negative consequences. However, the concern about cell phones and teens has been greatly exaggerated. As a tool for communication, information, and entertainment, cell phones have become a useful and important part of daily life for teens and adults alike.

Chapter Four

Is Cell Phone Addiction a Serious Problem?

Cell Phone Addiction Is a Serious Problem

- Like other addicts, people with an addiction to cell phones experience feelings of withdrawal and anxiety when separated from their phones.
- Cell phone addiction negatively impacts personal relationships, leading to a decline in intimacy and reduced participation in outside interests.
- Increasing use of cell phones can lead to nomophobia, an irrational fear of being separated from a mobile phone.

The Debate at a Glance

Worries About Cell Phone Addiction Are Exaggerated

- Unlike drug and alcohol addiction, the consequences of cell phone overuse are minimal.
- Cell phone overuse is not a disorder; rather, it is a symptom of an underlying mental health disorder.
- The increasing use of cell phones around the globe is an indication that they have become a modern necessity of life, not an addiction.

Cell Phone Addiction Is a Serious Problem

"We get some kind of reward from the use of our cell phone that produces pleasure—a lot of dopamine and serotonin in our brain—that keeps us coming back. So I think, and the research tells us, that behavioral addictions like cell phone addiction are just as real as substance addiction."

—James Roberts, a professor of marketing at Baylor University.

Quoted in Pam Harrison, "Overuse of Cell Phones: An Addiction Like Any Other?," Medscape.com, November 30, 2012. www.medscape.com.

Consider these questions as you read:

1. How persuasive is the argument that cell phone addiction is a serious problem? Which arguments are strongest, and why?
2. How can you tell if a person has a cell phone addiction?
3. Do you think that the consequences of cell phone addiction are as serious as the consequences of other addictions? Why or why not?

Editor's note: The discussion that follows presents common arguments made in support of this perspective, reinforced by facts, quotes, and examples taken from various sources.

In airplanes and doctors' offices, there are warnings to turn off cell phones and other electronic devices. Although many people power down without a second thought, there are a growing number of people who feel anxious about being without their cell phones. For these people, turning off the phone for even a few minutes can cause anxiety. As cell phone use increases, addiction to these devices is becoming a problem, one that can have unintended, serious consequences for those affected.

Cell Phone Use Can Be Addictive

For Californian Christiana Ike, being without a cell phone causes extreme anxiety. She copes by having three cell phones and makes sure that at least one is with her at all times, even in the shower. Ike also carries two phone chargers to make sure that she is never without power. "I'll have it sitting there on the counter, because I'm thinking, 'What if President Obama calls or the pope?' I don't know why I do that,"[59] Ike says. Like a growing number of users, Ike believes that she is addicted to her phone.

Although cell phone addiction is hard to define, mental health experts say that it is characterized by feelings of withdrawal, compulsive phone checking, and using the phone to make oneself feel better. "At first glance, one might have the tendency to dismiss such aberrant cell phone use as merely youthful nonsense—a passing fad," says James Roberts, a professor of marketing at Baylor University who conducted a study on cell phone addiction. "But an emerging body of literature has given increasing credence to cell phone addiction and similar behavioral addictions."[60]

Psychologists say that cell phone addiction is similar to other behavioral addictions, such as compulsive shopping, gambling, and compulsive eating. It can be as serious as substance addictions. "People understand substance addictions. They understand that we can take a drug that impacts parts of our brain and reinforces the pleasure principle, so we're addicted to that particular substance. But it's no different with behavioral addiction,"[61] says Roberts.

A cell phone user who feels the need to check his or her phone for updates and messages continuously—and cannot be away from the phone even for a few minutes—may be experiencing the same chemical changes in the brain that other addicts experience. "For some people who use the phone excessively, we know that the brain is actually responding to the phone as if it is a drug," says Elizabeth Waterman, a clinical psychologist at the Morningside Recovery Center in Costa Mesa, California, which runs a cell phone addiction support group. "So there's some burst of dopamine that occurs when the person can engage in the pleasurable behavior." Waterman says that cell phone users have become conditioned to check their phones all day long. "They have an anxiety response when their phone is inaccessible and they engage in desperate behaviors to avoid losing their phone,"[62] she says.

The Effects on Personal Relationships

Like other addictions, cell phone and texting addictions can negatively affect a user's personal and work relationships. Addicts become so focused on their phones that they pay less attention to or ignore family, friends, and even work. In a study conducted at England's Staffordshire University, 7 percent of participants reported that their use of mobile phones caused them to lose a relationship or job.

Like any addictive behavior, cell phone and texting addictions can negatively affect quality of life. "It's an opportunity cost," says James Roberts, "so we are crowding out so many more important activities, including family and friends and other pursuits that might bring us true happiness."[63]

> "For some people who use the phone excessively, we know that the brain is actually responding to the phone as if it is a drug."[62]
>
> —Elizabeth Waterman, a clinical psychologist at the Morningside Recovery Center in Costa Mesa, California.

Christiana Ike admits that her cell phone addiction has affected her personal relationships. "If someone has to talk to me, it's hard for them to pry me away from my phone especially if I have a message," she says. "I have had several people try and take my phone away from me or tell me I'm being disrespectful and rude. Unfortunately I become so attached to communicating with everybody via my iPhone, that I become less attached to people who are physically in front of me. And that's where it becomes detrimental,"[64] Ike says.

In 2012 University of Essex researchers reported that the mere presence of a cell phone can negatively affect a user's interactions with other people. In their study, the researchers asked pairs of strangers to sit together in a booth for ten minutes and share a personal story. In each booth, either a notebook or a cell phone was placed in the participants' peripheral vision. Later, in response to questions from the researchers, the pairs

Cell Phone Use Damages Relationships

One of the barometers of addiction is whether the behavior disrupts or damages relationships with other people. In a 2012 survey, a significant number of cell phone users from several countries agree that their phones have caused problems in relationships with spouses, family, and friends.

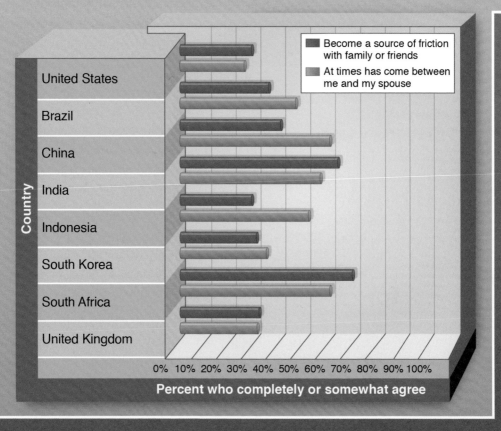

Percent who completely or somewhat agree

Legend:
- Become a source of friction with family or friends
- At times has come between me and my spouse

Country (top to bottom): United States, Brazil, China, India, Indonesia, South Korea, South Africa, United Kingdom

Source: Qualcomm, "Poll Results: *Time* Mobility Poll, in Cooperation with Qualcomm," August 2012. www.qualcomm.com.

who had a phone within sight reported feeling less close to each other and having a lower quality of relationship than the pairs who did not have a phone in their booth. "We found evidence [mobile phones] can have negative effects on closeness, connection, and conversation quality. These results demonstrate that the presence of mobile phones can interfere with human relationships,"[65] wrote the study researchers.

Separation Phobia

Some users have become so dependent on their cell phones that they have developed an unhealthy phobia about being away from their phones. Mary Helen Beatificato from Boston, Massachusetts, cannot stand to be separated from her cell phone. "The panic and anxiety that I have during those seconds is probably not normal," she says. "Even while I'm sleeping, my hand is on my phone." Beatificato is so attached to her phone, she takes it everywhere. "It goes with me in the bath and the shower. I actually have a case that is fully submergible,"[66] she says.

> "Unfortunately I become so attached to communicating with everybody via my iPhone, that I become less attached to people who are physically in front of me. And that's where it becomes detrimental."[64]
>
> —Christiana Ike, a cell phone addict.

Mental health experts have given Beatificato's abnormal attachment to her phone a name—*nomophobia*, from the phrase "no mobile phone." British researchers first used the term *nomophobia* in 2008 to describe people who experience anxiety when they are not connected to mobile technology or mobile phones. Mental health experts say that people who suffer from nomophobia feel like they cannot turn their phones off and obsess about having enough battery power. They constantly check for e-mails, text messages, and missed calls.

In recent years nomophobia has become a real and serious problem. According to a 2012 survey of one thousand people conducted by Internet security and mobile technology firm SecurEnvoy, 66 percent reported that they experienced real fear when thinking about losing their phones and being disconnected. People aged eighteen to twenty-four were the most at risk for nomophobia, with 77 percent saying they were uncomfortable being separated from their cell phone for more than a few minutes.

For those affected, nomophobia can cause many problems in daily life, including damaging personal relationships and disrupting activities at school and in the workplace. "It also becomes a problem if you're getting in trouble at work or at school because you're looking at non-work and non-school messages or material on your phone,"[67] says Waterman of the Morningside Recovery Center. Some experts say that people with nomophobia may also be more vulnerable to other addictions, such as using marijuana or alcohol, because these substances help them cope with the anxiety they feel regarding their phones.

Morningside runs a recovery group for people with nomophobia—possibly the first such group in the United States. The group helps people recognize the signs and symptoms of their dependency on mobile technology. It also teaches them emotional, cognitive, and behavioral techniques to help them break out of their addiction. Clients are first taught healthy coping skills to manage the anxiety they feel when their phones are taken away, Waterman says. "We help them identify irrational fears associated with the phone loss and help them create new rational thoughts to replace those fears," she says. "We teach them distraction skills, so they can learn to distract themselves with healthier behaviors instead of engaging in the addictive behavior."[68]

Every year more people are spending time on cell phones, making calls, sending texts, or going online. For some, the phone has become more than a tool; it has become something they literally cannot live without. For these people, their attachment to their phones has become a serious problem that can damage many areas of their lives.

Worries About Cell Phone Addiction Are Exaggerated

"While the fact that so many people say they experience real fear just thinking about losing their mobile phone is startling, it doesn't necessarily mean that every one of those of 66% of respondents need treatment."

—Elizabeth Waterman, a clinical psychologist with Morningside Recovery Center in California.

Quoted in Michele Lerner, "Nomophobia: Is Your Cellphone Addiction Covered?," Fox Business, December 19, 2012. www.foxbusiness.com.

Consider these questions as you read:

1. How persuasive is the argument that cell phone addiction is not a serious problem? Which arguments are strongest, and why?
2. Do you believe that cell phone overuse is a true addiction? Why or why not?
3. Do you think that cell phones are a necessity or a luxury? Why?

Editor's note: The discussion that follows presents common arguments made in support of this perspective, reinforced by facts, quotes, and examples taken from various sources.

A person who constantly talks, texts, or checks messages on a cell phone might be rude or annoying, but characterizing that behavior as addiction goes too far. The addiction label should be reserved for serious problems—drug abuse, compulsive gambling, alcoholism. Instead of addiction treatment, people who are constantly on their phones may best benefit from an old-fashioned lesson on manners.

The Consequences of Cell Phone Overuse Are Minor

Real addictions usually have damaging consequences—to both physical and mental health. People who are addicted to drugs or alcohol can experience acute physical effects such as increased heart rate, impaired muscle control, dizziness, vomiting, and loss of consciousness. Substance addictions also affect the mind, leading to poor decision making, loss of concentration, lowered inhibitions, and exaggerated emotions. In some cases, long-term abuse of drugs and alcohol can permanently damage organs and lead to overdose and death. Drugs and alcohol impair relationships with other people, and they frequently cause addicts to lose friends, family, and jobs. Behavioral addictions such as gambling can lead to the loss of a home and a job as well as seriously damaging relationships.

In contrast, people who spend too much time on their cell phones rarely experience serious medical problems or lose their homes or jobs as a result of their cell phone use. Instead, they may only damage personal relationships or spend less time on other activities, neither of which is life threatening. Because the consequences from excessive use of cell phones are significantly less severe than those associated with traditional substance or behavioral addictions, some mental health experts believe cell phone overuse should not be viewed as addiction. "To consider something as a disorder or illness, the behavior must impair one's life significantly. And at this moment, we do not see these dramatic consequences [from excessive cell phone use] in a large population," says Zsolt Demetrovics, the editor of the *Journal of Addictive Behaviors*. Demetrovics believes that behaviors that do not have serious consequences, such as cell phone overuse, should be examined, "but we should not overdramatize them as serious illnesses,"[69] he says.

> "To consider something as a disorder or illness, the behavior must impair one's life significantly. And at this moment, we do not see these dramatic consequences [from excessive cell phone use] in a large population."[69]
>
> —Zsolt Demetrovics, the editor of the *Journal of Addictive Behaviors*.

Just because some people experience anxiety when they do not have access to mobile technology does not mean they have an addiction. "Addiction is a serious thing, and it's important not to trivialize it the way some people do when they say they are 'addicted' to a TV show or to

Necessity Does Not Equal Addiction

Among young adults, cell phones have overtaken landlines as a necessary feature of modern life. This finding, revealed in a 2010 Pew Research Center survey, does not in any way suggest that this group has an addiction to their phones—nor should it. Cell phones, like computers and cars, are simply part of modern life.

Landline Phone vs. Cell Phone

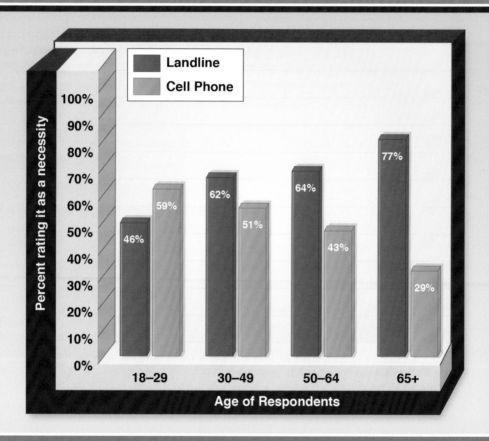

Source: Paul Taylor and Wendy Wang, "The Fading Glory of the Television and Telephone," Pew Research Social and Demographic Trends, August 19, 2010. www.pewsocialtrends.org.

chocolate. By definition, addiction occurs when someone experiences repeated harm from 'x' or whatever it is they are addicted to, which is usually something enjoyable,"[70] says Brian Johnson, the director of addiction psychiatry at the State University of New York Upstate Medical School in Syracuse, New York. The harm in using a cell phone excessively is minor compared to the real-life consequences of substance abuse or gambling. Therefore, it is a mistake to label cell phone overuse as an addiction.

The Underlying Disorders Are the Real Culprit

For people around the world, mobile technology is a convenience that makes daily tasks easier. When mobile technology becomes more of a hindrance than a help, it is probably because the user suffers from anxiety, obsessive-compulsive disorder, or some other condition that has nothing to do with having a phone. These disorders can cause users to compulsively check their phones for voicemails and text messages. "When (cell phone overuse) really becomes problematic for a lot of people is if they have underlying anxiety or depression," says Lisa Merlo, an assistant professor of psychiatry in the University of Florida's College of Medicine. "This can really exacerbate it or (cause) their symptoms to manifest themselves,"[71] says Merlo. For example, people who worry about how others perceive them may become easily agitated if their phone calls, texts, or e-mails are not returned immediately. They may obsessively check their phones until the message has been answered. This type of problem will be apparent in many areas of their lives, not just in connection with their phone.

The cell phone itself is often not the problem. Usually it is a symptom of a larger issue. Elizabeth Waterman is a clinical psychologist at the Morningside Recovery Center in California. The center treats a wide variety of conditions, including addictions and mental health conditions. Although the center has a program that specializes in cell phone addiction and nomophobia—the fear of being without a mobile phone—Waterman says that people who have a problem with cell phone overuse often have an underlying disorder. "People don't typically come to us for treatment just because of their addiction to their cell phone," says Waterman. "Usually there's a dual problem such as substance abuse or mental illness coupled with nomophobia. Often nomophobia is part of a generalized anxiety problem. For example, one patient we're working with has post-traumatic stress disorder and a significant fear of losing her phone."[72]

A Modern Necessity, Not an Addiction

The increasing use of cell phones and other mobile technology across society does not necessarily mean that there is a serious, growing addiction to phones. It more likely indicates that cell phones have become an integral part of modern life—much like a car or refrigerator or computer. According to a 2012 Pew Internet & American Life Project, 88 percent of American adults have a cell phone, increased from 53 percent in 2000. In addition, 46 percent of American adults own a smartphone. In today's hectic world, people are using their phones as minicomputers, planners, and entertainment devices. From their phones, they coordinate busy family schedules, check messages while on the go, get news reports, bank online, play games, and listen to music.

> "Often nomophobia is part of a generalized anxiety problem."[72]
>
> —Elizabeth Waterman, a clinical psychologist at the Morningside Recovery Center in California.

When cell phones were first introduced, many people considered them to be luxury items that were nice to have but not needed. Yet as cell phones have grown in functionality and have become more integrated into daily life, more people view them as a necessity. And as often happens with new technology, cell phones are replacing old technology. Research has shown that cell phones are slowly replacing landline phones as a necessity of life. In a nationwide survey from the Pew Research Center's Social & Demographic Trends project, the percent of Americans who view the landline phone as a necessity of life dropped from 68 percent in 2009 to 62 percent in 2010. At the same time, almost half of the survey respondents said that cell phones were a necessity. For younger Americans, landline phones are becoming even less important as they spend less time talking on the phone and more time texting. For survey respondents ages eighteen to twenty-nine years old, fewer than half (46 percent) said that the landline phone was a necessity of life.

Today there are more cell phones in the United States than landline phones. Some people are even giving up their landline phones entirely and replacing them with cell phones. According to a Pew Research Center analysis of government data, the number of US households that have a landline phone has dropped from 97 percent in 2001 to 74 percent in 2010. In addition, approximately 25 percent of households own cell phones exclusively and do not have a landline phone.

Cell phones have dramatically changed the way people communicate, entertain, and go online. More people are using cell phones for a variety of functions, from texting to reading books. Although some people warn that increasing cell phone use is a significant problem, these concerns have been exaggerated. People are attached to their cell phones but not because of an unhealthy addiction; instead, it is because cell phones have become an integral tool for daily life.

Source Notes

Overview: The Mobile Life

1. Quoted in Michael Inbar, "Parents of Teen Who Died Texting and Driving: 'Kids Think They're Invincible,'" Today.com, March 5, 2012. www.today.com.
2. Quoted in Inbar, "Parents of Teen Who Died Texting and Driving."
3. Quoted in *Salt Lake Tribune,* "Idaho Police: USU Student Texting Before Fatal Crash," February 9, 2012. www.sltrib.com.
4. Quoted in Emiley Morgan, "Death of USU Student in Idaho Points to Risks of Distracted Driving," *Deseret News,* January 17, 2012. www.deseretnews.com.
5. Quoted in Cyrus Farivar, "Talk Is Cheap: Cell Phones Hit Six Billion Worldwide," ARS Technica, October 11, 2012. http://arstechnica.com.
6. Quoted in Andrew Beaujon, "Pew: 82% Use Cell Phones to Take Pictures," Poynter Institute, November 26, 2012. www.poynter.org.
7. Nancy Gibbs, "Your Life Is Fully Mobile," Time.com, August 16, 2012. http://techland.time.com.

Chapter One: Are Stronger Laws Needed to Prevent Cell Phone Use by Drivers?

8. Quoted in Emiley Morgan, "Death of USU Student in Idaho Points to Risks of Distracted Driving."
9. California Office of Traffic Safety, "Cell Phone Distracted Driving Deaths Down Since Laws Enacted," March 5, 2012. www.ots.ca.gov.
10. Quoted in EIN News, "Cell Phone Ban Study Shows Reduction in California Fatal Car Accidents," March 30, 2012. http://uspolitics.einnews.com.
11. Quoted in Scott Neuman, "Experts Question Need for Stronger Cellphone Ban," NPR, December 14, 2011. www.npr.org.

12. Quoted in NorthJersey.com, "NJ Panel Approves Tougher Driver Cellphone Law," June 4, 2012. www.northjersey.com.

13. Quoted in CBSNews.com, "Hands-Free Phones Just as Risky, Research Shows," December 15, 2011. www.cbsnews.com.

14. Quoted in National Safety Council, "The National Safety Council Releases White Paper on Brain Distraction During Cell Phone Use While Driving," March 26, 2010. www.nsc.org.

15. Quoted in Sarah Kliff, "Would a National Ban on Cellphones While Driving Make Us Safer? Probably Not," *Wonkblog* (blog), December 13, 2011. www.washingtonpost.com.

16. Quoted in CBS Baltimore, "Md. Officials Look to Ban Handheld Cell Phones While Driving," February 11, 2012. http://baltimore .cbslocal.com.

17. Quoted in CBS Baltimore, "Md. Officials Look to Ban Handheld Cell Phones While Driving."

18. Quoted in *Boston Globe,* "It's Not the Cell Phone, but the Driver That's High-Risk," August 26, 2012. www.boston.com.

19. Quoted in Neuman, "Experts Question Need for Stronger Cellphone Ban."

20. Quoted in Neuman, "Experts Question Need for Stronger Cellphone Ban."

21. Quoted in Morgan, "Death of USU Student in Idaho Points to Risks of Distracted Driving."

22. Quoted in University of Illinois, "Study: Cellphone Bans Associated with Fewer Urban Accidents," November 15, 2012. http://news .illinois.edu.

23. Quoted in University of Illinois, "Study."

24. Insurance Institute for Highway Safety, "Highway Loss Data Institute Bulletin: Texting Laws and Collision Claim Frequency," September 2010. www.iihs.org.

25. Quoted in Ken Leiser, "Study: Risk-Taking Drivers Don't Stop with Cell Phones," *St. Louis Post-Dispatch*, January 25, 2013. www.stlto day.com.

26. Quoted in *Boston Globe,* "It's Not the Cell Phone, but the Driver That's High-Risk."

27. Quoted in *Boston Globe,* "It's Not the Cell Phone, but the Driver That's High-Risk."

28. Quoted in Leiser, "Study."

Chapter Two: Do Cell Phones Pose a Health Hazard?

29. Quoted in Danielle Dellorto, "WHO: Cell Phone Use Can Increase Possible Cancer Risk," CNN.com, May 31, 2011. www.cnn.com.

30. Quoted in Tara Parker-Pope, "Questions About Cellphones and Brain Tumors," *Well* (blog), May 18, 2010. http://well.blogs.nytimes.com.

31. Quoted in Dellorto, "WHO."

32. Quoted in Laurie Tarkan, "Cell Phones May Damage Sperm, Health Advocacy Group Says," FoxNews.com, July 5, 2012. www.foxnews.com.

33. Quoted in Tarkan, "Cell Phones May Damage Sperm, Health Advocacy Group Says."

34. Quoted in Science*Daily*, "Cell Phone Use in Pregnancy May Cause Behavioral Disorders in Offspring, Mouse Study Suggests," March 15, 2012. www.sciencedaily.com.

35. Quoted in Science*Daily*, "Cell Phone Use in Pregnancy May Cause Behavioral Disorders in Offspring, Mouse Study Suggests."

36. Quoted in Lia Steakley, "Stanford Neurologist Comments on the Health Risks of Mobile Phones," *Scope* (blog), November 26, 2012. http://scopeblog.stanford.edu.

37. Federal Communications Commission, "Radio Frequency Safety." http://transition.fcc.gov.

38. Norwegian Institute of Public Health, "Mobile Phones and Wireless Networks: No Evidence of Health Risk Found," September 12, 2012. www.fhi.no.

39. Quoted in Ian Sample, "Mobile Phone Study Finds No Solid Link to Brain Tumours," *Guardian*, May 17, 2010. www.guardian.co.uk.

40. Quoted in WDAY News, "Debate on Whether Cell Phones Can Cause Cancer Continues," June 13, 2012. www.wday.com.

41. Quoted in Lea Winerman, "Study: Cell Phone Radiation Stirs Brain Activity, but Health Effects Unknown," PBS.org, February 22, 2011. www.pbs.org.

42. Quoted in CBS News, "CDC: Majority of Older Teens Text While Driving," CBSNews.com, June 7, 2012. www.cbsnews.com.

43. Quoted in *USA Today*, "CDC: Older Teens Often Text While Behind the Wheel," June 7, 2012. http://usatoday30.usatoday.com.

44. Raychelle Cassada Lohmann, "The Dangers of Teen Sexting," *Teen Angst* (blog), July 20, 2012. www.psychologytoday.com.

45. Quoted in Julielynn Wong, "Sexting Linked to Increased Sexual Activity in Teens," ABC News, September 17, 2012. http://abcnews.go.com.

46. Quoted in Nicole Vap and Kevin Torres, "Two Teens Charged in Standley Lake High Sexting Incident," 9News.com, April 10, 2012. www.9news.com.

47. Quoted in Graeme Hamilton, "Amanda Todd and the Greatly Exaggerated Cyber-Bullying Plague: Web Harassment Not on the Rise, Researcher Says," *National Post*, October 26, 2012. http://news.nationalpost.com.

48. Quoted in Jennifer Ludden, "Teen Texting Soars; Will Social Skills Suffer?," NPR, April 20, 2010. www.npr.org.

49. Quoted in Lauren Barack, "High School Students Use Cell Phones in Class—but Not for Schoolwork, Says Study," *School Library Journal*, January 7, 2013. www.thedigitalshift.com.

50. Quoted in Hamilton, "Amanda Todd and the Greatly Exaggerated Cyber-Bullying Plague."

51. Quoted in Salynn Boyles, "Study: Fears of Teen 'Sexting' May Be Exaggerated," WebMD, December 5, 2011. www.webmd.com.

52. Quoted in Wong, "Sexting Linked to Increased Sexual Activity in Teens."

53. Quoted in Donna St. George, "Study of Teen Cellphone Use Reinforces Impression That They're Always Using Them," *Washington Post*, April 20, 2010. www.washingtonpost.com.

54. Quoted in St. George, "Study of Teen Cellphone Use Reinforces Impression That They're Always Using Them."

55. Quoted in St. George, "Study of Teen Cellphone Use Reinforces Impression That They're Always Using Them."

56. Quoted in Audrey Watters, "What Tech in Schools Really Looks Like," *Digital Shift*, April 30, 2012. www.thedigitalshift.com.

57. Kathryn Zickuhr and Aaron Smith, "Digital Differences," Pew Internet & American Life Project, April 13, 2012. http://pewinternet.org.

58. Quoted in St. George, "Study of Teen Cellphone Use Reinforces Impression That They're Always Using Them."

Chapter Four: Is Cell Phone Addiction a Serious Problem?

59. Quoted in Daisy Lin and Bruce Hensel, "Are You Addicted to Your Cell Phone?," NBC Los Angeles, November 1, 2012. www.nbclos angeles.com.

60. Quoted in *Huffington Post*, "Cell Phone Addiction Driven by Impulsivity, Materialism: Study," November 29, 2012. www.huffington post.com.

61. Quoted in Pam Harrison, "Overuse of Cell Phones: An Addiction Like Any Other?," Medscape, November 30, 2012. www.medscape.com.

62. Quoted in Lin and Hensel, "Are You Addicted to Your Cell Phone?"

63. Quoted in Harrison, "Overuse of Cell Phones."

64. Quoted in Lin and Hensel, "Are You Addicted to Your Cell Phone?"

65. Andrew K. Przybylski and Netta Weinstein, "Can You Connect with Me Now? How the Presence of Mobile Communication Technology Influences Face-to-Face Conversation Quality," *Journal of Social and Personal Relationships*, July 19, 2012. http://spr.sagepub.com.

66. Quoted in CBS Baltimore, "Mobile Phone Addiction Serious for Some," December 4, 2012. http://baltimore.cbslocal.com.

67. Quoted in Michele Lerner, "Nomophobia: Is Your Cellphone Addiction Covered?," Fox Business, December 19, 2012. www.foxbusiness.com.

68. Quoted in Lin and Hensel, "Are You Addicted to Your Cell Phone?"

69. Quoted in Harrison, "Overuse of Cell Phones."

70. Quoted in Lerner, "Nomophobia."

71. Quoted in Phys.org, "Addicted to Phones? Cell Phone Use Becoming a Major Problem for Some, Expert Says," January 18, 2007. http://phys.org.

72. Quoted in Lerner, "Nomophobia."

Cell Phone Facts

Cell Phones and Driving

- According to the CDC, 25 percent of drivers in the United States reported that they talk on their cell phone regularly or fairly often while driving.
- Drivers who use handheld devices are four times more likely to get into crashes serious enough to injure themselves, reports Monash University.
- According to researchers at the Virginia Tech Transportation Institute, text messaging creates a crash risk twenty-three times worse than driving while not distracted.
- The Virginia Tech Transportation Institute also reports that sending or receiving a text takes a driver's eyes from the road for an average of 4.6 seconds, which is the equivalent of driving the length of a football field blind at 55 miles per hour (89 km/h).
- Researchers at Carnegie Mellon University report that driving while using a cell phone reduces the amount of brain activity associated with driving by 37 percent.
- According Distraction.gov, at any given moment during daylight hours, more than eight hundred thousand vehicles are being driven by someone using a handheld cell phone.

Cell Phone Usage

- According to CTIA, more than 196 billion text messages were sent or received in the United States in June 2011, up nearly 50 percent from June 2009.
- As of December 2012, the Pew Internet & American Life Project reports that 87 percent of American adults own a cell phone, and 45 percent have a smartphone.
- According to a 2012 survey by the Pew Internet & American Life Project, smartphone owners report that they use their phones to check the

weather (77 percent), check social networking sites (68 percent), get directions (65 percent), get news (64 percent), play games (64 percent), and upload photos (58 percent).

Teens and Cell Phones

- According to the Pew Research Center, 40 percent of American teens say they have been in a car when the driver used a cell phone in a way that put people in danger.
- Twenty-seven percent of teens use their cell phones to go online, reports the Internet safety and education organization Web Wise Kids.
- A 2010 Pew survey found that 75 percent of twelve- to seventeen-year-olds have cell phones.
- According to Pew Research, 83 percent of teens use their phones to take pictures, 64 percent share pictures with others, 60 percent play music on their phones, and 46 percent play games on their phones.
- The typical teen sends and receives about one hundred texts per day, according to the CDC.
- The research advisory firm mobileYouth reports that, given the choice, teens would choose to spend their last ten dollars on their cell phones rather than on food.

Cell Phone Attachment

- According to a recent survey by the Pew Internet & American Life Project, 67 percent of cell owners find themselves checking their phone for messages, alerts, or calls—even when they do not notice their phone ringing or vibrating. Some 18 percent of cell owners say that they do this frequently.
- According to the Pew Internet & American Life Project, 44 percent of cell owners have slept with their phone next to their bed because they wanted to make sure they did not miss any calls, text messages, or other updates during the night.
- Twenty-nine percent of cell owners describe their cell phone as "something they can't imagine living without," reports the Pew Internet & American Life Project.

Related Organizations and Websites

Centers for Disease Control and Prevention (CDC)
1600 Clifton Rd.
Atlanta, GA 30333
phone: (800) CDC-INFO
website: www.cdc.gov

The CDC works with partners around the country and the world to monitor health, detect and investigate health problems, conduct research into health issues, and promote healthy behaviors, including those related to cell phone use.

CTIA
1400 Sixteenth St. NW, Suite 600
Washington, DC 20036
phone: (202) 736-3200 • fax: (202) 785-0721
website: www.ctia.org

Founded in 1984, this international nonprofit membership organization supports the wireless communications industry and provides information on cell phone–related issues and laws.

Cyberbullying Research Center
website: www.cyberbullying.us

The Cyberbullying Research Center provides up-to-date information about the nature, extent, causes, and consequences of cyberbullying among teens.

Distraction.gov
National Highway Traffic Safety Administration
1200 New Jersey Ave., SE

Washington, DC 20590

phone: (888) 327-4236

website: www.distraction.gov

Distraction.gov is the official US government website from the National Highway Traffic Safety Administration focused on the issue of distracted driving. The site offers up-to-date information, facts, and statistics regarding distracted driving, including the use of cell phones.

Don't Drive and Text

222 N. Main St., Suite A

Bryan, TX 77803

website: http://dontdriveandtext.org

This organization provides information on the dangers of texting and driving in order to educate people about the practice.

Morningside Recovery Center

3421 Via Oporto, Suite 200

Newport Beach, CA 92663

phone: (949) 675-0006 • fax: (949) 675-0007

Morningside Recovery Center has several locations in California and runs a cell phone addiction support group, along with other groups and treatment services for people suffering from chemical dependency or mental health disorders.

Pew Research Center

1615 L St. NW, Suite 700

Washington, DC 20036

phone: (202) 419-4500 • fax: (202) 419-4505

website: www.pewinternet.org

The Pew Research Center conducts and analyzes the results of public opinion polls and studies on a variety of issues. The Pew Internet & American Life Project addresses the impact of the Internet on American life and society and has studied cell phone use.

Text Free Driving Organization
website: www.textfreedriving.org

This group is dedicated to raising awareness of the dangers of texting while driving and works to support laws that would eliminate cell phone use while driving.

US Food and Drug Administration (FDA)
10903 New Hampshire Ave.
Silver Spring, MD 20993
phone: (888) INFO-FDA
website: www.fda.gov

The FDA is an agency of the US Department of Health and Human Services. It is responsible for protecting and promoting public health and has addressed safety issues related to cell phone radiation.

Virginia Tech Transportation Institute
3500 Transportation Research Plaza
Blacksburg, VA 24061
phone: (540) 231-1500 • fax: (540) 231-1555
website: www.vtti.vt.edu

The institute conducts research aimed at saving lives, time, and money in the transportation field, including research on the use of cell phones and driving.

World Health Organization (WHO)
Avenue Appia 20
1211 Geneva 27, Switzerland
phone: 41 22 791 21 11 • fax: 41 22 791 31 11
website: www.who.int

WHO supports research and provides information on a wide variety of health issues, including those related to cell phone use.

For Further Research

Books

Brian X. Chen, *Always On: How the iPhone Unlocked the Anything-Anytime-Anywhere Future—and Locked Us In*. Cambridge, MA: Da Capo, 2011.

Devra Davis, *Disconnect: The Truth About Cell Phone Radiation, What the Industry Has Done to Hide It, and How to Protect Your Family*. New York: Dutton, 2010.

Stefan Kiesbye, *Cell Phones and Driving*. Farmington Hills, MI: Greenhaven, 2010.

Patricia D. Netzley, *How Does Cell Phone Use Impact Teenagers?* San Diego: ReferencePoint, 2013.

Michele Sequeira, *Cell Phone Science: What Happens When You Call and Why*. Albuquerque: University of New Mexico Press, 2010.

Bonnie Szumski and Jill Karson, *Are Cell Phones Dangerous?* San Diego: ReferencePoint, 2011.

Internet Sources

Nancy V. Gifford, *Sexting in the U.S.A.*, Family Online Safety Institute. www.fosi.org.

Jennifer A. Hanley, *Cyberbullying: A Global Concern*, Family Online Safety Institute. www.fosi.org.

Amanda Lenhart et al., *Teens and Mobile Phones*, Pew Internet & American Life Project, April 20, 2010. www.pewinternet.org.

Mary Madden et al., *Teens and Technology 2013*, Pew Internet & American Life Project, March 13, 2013. www.pewinternet.org.

Aaron Smith, *Best and Worst of the Mobile Community*, Pew Internet & American Life Project, November 30, 2012. www.pewinternet.org.

World Health Organization, *Mobile Phone Use: A Growing Problem of Driver Distraction*, 2011. www.who.int.

Index

About the Author

Carla Mooney is the author of many books for young adults and children. She lives in Pittsburgh, Pennsylvania, with her husband and three children.